Bill and Melinda Gates

JOSH GREGORY

Children's Press®
An Imprint of Scholastic Inc.
New York   Toronto   London   Auckland   Sydney
Mexico City   New Delhi   Hong Kong
Danbury, Connecticut

Content Consultant
James Marten, PhD
Professor and Chair, History Department
Marquette University
Milwaukee, Wisconsin

Library of Congress Cataloging-in Publication Data

Gregory, Josh.
 Bill and Melinda Gates/Josh Gregory.
    p. cm.—(A true book)
 Includes bibliographical references and index.
  ISBN 978-0-531-21905-8 (lib. bdg.) — ISBN 978-0-531-23876-9 (pbk.)
1. Gates, Bill, 1955– Juvenile literature. 2. Gates, Melinda, 1964—Juvenile literature.
3. Businesspeople—United States—Biography—Juvenile literature. 4. Computer software industry—United States—History—Juvenile literature. 5. Microsoft Corporation—History—Juvenile literature. 6. Bill & Melinda Gates Foundation—History—Juvenile literature. I. Title.
  HD9696.63.U62G37443 2013
  338.7'610040922—dc23 [B]   2012036002

All rights reserved. Published in 2013 by Children's Press, an imprint of Scholastic Inc.
Printed in the United States of America 113
SCHOLASTIC, CHILDREN'S PRESS, A TRUE BOOK™, and associated logos are trademarks and/or registered trademarks of Scholastic Inc.
1 2 3 4 5 6 7 8 9 10 R 22 21 20 19 18 17 16 15 14 13

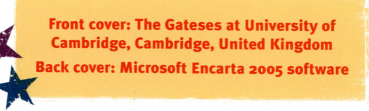

Front cover: The Gateses at University of Cambridge, Cambridge, United Kingdom
Back cover: Microsoft Encarta 2005 software

Find the Truth!

Everything you are about to read is true *except* for one of the sentences on this page.

Which one is **TRUE**?

T or F   Bill and Melinda Gates started Microsoft together.

T or F   The Bill and Melinda Gates Foundation is the largest charitable foundation in the world.

Find the answers in this book.

Contents

THE BIG TRUTH!

Bill Gates has long been a major player in the computer industry.

The Gateses support HIV/AIDS prevention programs in India.

CHAPTER 1

A Young Genius

On October 28, 1955, William and Mary Gates welcomed their second child into the world. They named the boy William Henry Gates III, after his father and grandfather. Growing up, most people called him Bill. Bill was a fast learner and was always interested in learning new things. However, his parents may never have imagined that he would one day change the world with his incredible inventions and generous charity work.

One of the Gateses' goals in India is to stop the spread of polio.

The Gates Family

Bill Gates was born and raised in Seattle, Washington. He had an older sister named Kristianne and a younger sister named Libby. His family was wealthy. Bill's grandfather was a banker. His father was a lawyer.

As a result, the family lived a comfortable lifestyle. Bill's mother was very generous with the family's money. She donated to many causes and spent time working for many charitable organizations.

Bill read a full set of encyclopedias before he was nine years old.

Seattle's Space Needle and other famous landmarks were built for the 1962 World's Fair.

A Lifetime of Learning

Even as a very young child, Bill loved reading and finding out about new things. He was six years old when he first saw a computer. Along with millions of other people, he visited the 1962 World's Fair in Seattle. The fair had an exhibit in which some of the most advanced computers of the time were on display. They were big enough to fill entire rooms.

Bill returned to Lakeside School in 2005 to give a speech to the students.

Bill graduated from Lakeside School.

A New School

When Bill was 12 years old, his parents decided to enroll him in the nearby Lakeside School. Lakeside was a private school that offered resources that other schools did not. One of these resources was a computer system.

Bill soon began teaching himself how to write computer programs, or software. During his high school years, he formed a computer club. The members called themselves the Lakeside Programmers.

Paul Allen

One of Bill's closest friends in the Lakeside Programmers was Paul Allen. Like Bill, Paul was born and raised in Seattle and had a knack for creating new software. In high school, the two friends worked together to build and sell some useful programs. One of their programs recorded information about traffic in Seattle. Another helped Lakeside build class schedules for its students. Bill and Paul's remarkable partnership would continue for many years.

On to Harvard

In 1973, Bill graduated from Lakeside School. He set off for Harvard University in Massachusetts to study pre-law before attending law school. Though he was far from home, one of Gates's best friends was nearby. Paul Allen had been hired at a technology company near Harvard. One day during Gates's sophomore year, Allen told him about a new computer called the Altair 8800. It was small, yet powerful. However, the Altair had no software.

Harvard University is a prestigious school located in Cambridge, Massachusetts.

The Altair 8800 did not come with a keyboard or monitor.

Building a New BASIC

A person uses commands in a computer's programming language to "tell" a computer to perform certain tasks. Gates and Allen began adapting a language called BASIC to run on the Altair 8800. Their new version could be used to build software for the Altair and make the computer easier to use. The two young programmers made a deal with MITS, the company that made the Altair. Their version of BASIC would come with each computer sold.

MS-BASIC was a huge success on the Altair 8800.

Creating a Company

Leaders at MITS were so impressed with the program
that they offered Allen a job. He left Massachusetts in
1975 to work at MITS in Albuquerque, New Mexico. That
summer, Gates flew there to join him. The friends started
a company and named it Microsoft, a combination of
microcomputer and *software*. Gates and Allen had kept
the legal right to sell their version of BASIC, called
MS-BASIC, to anyone. As a result, Microsoft could
license MS-BASIC to additional companies.

Full Time

Gates returned to Massachusetts in the fall to begin his junior year of college. But he and Allen both found themselves spending more and more time doing work for Microsoft. Soon, Allen quit his job at MITS. Gates dropped out of college. Both began to work full-time at Microsoft.

They found office space for their company in Albuquerque. They also began hiring employees. Microsoft was officially up and running.

Starting Microsoft was the first step to making Bill Gates a household name.

Gates (left) and Allen's (right)
new company grew quickly.

CHAPTER 2

From Innovator to Billionaire

Microsoft continued to find success licensing MS-BASIC to other computer manufacturers. In 1979, Gates and Allen moved their offices to Bellevue, Washington. The following year, leading computer manufacturer IBM contacted Microsoft. The company asked Microsoft to develop an **operating system** for its upcoming computers. Gates agreed but insisted that Microsoft keep the legal right to license his software to other computer companies in addition to IBM.

Good News and Bad News

The resulting software, Microsoft Disk Operating System (MS-DOS), was released in 1981. It was Microsoft's biggest success yet. MS-DOS came with every IBM computer sold. Because Microsoft could license the software to anyone, MS-DOS also came with many other companies' computers.

In 1983, Paul Allen was diagnosed with cancer. As a result, he gave up most of his responsibilities at Microsoft. Gates was sorry to see his friend go but continued to push Microsoft forward.

MS-DOS used text commands, typed in with a keyboard, to control a computer's operations.

```
MS-DOS version 1.25
Copyright 1981,82 Computer, Inc.

Command v. 1.1
Current date is Tue 1-01-1980
Enter new date:
Current time is 1:01:56.20
```

18

Windows helped make computers easier to use for the average person.

Looking Through Windows

In 1985, Microsoft released a new operating system called Windows. Unlike MS-DOS and other earlier operating systems, it was not based on text commands. Users once had to type in text commands to control their computers. Windows instead had a graphical user **interface**. This meant that users could operate a mouse to select and drag graphics called icons around a "desktop" on-screen. This made it easier for beginners to use computers.

Microsoft released its first laptop computer in 1986.

Billionaire Bill

Windows was a huge success. By 1986, Microsoft had outgrown its office in Bellevue. Gates constructed a massive new office compound in the nearby city of Redmond.

Microsoft had made Bill Gates a very rich man. In 1987, his personal fortune passed $1 billion. Gates did not let his success slow him down. That same year, Microsoft released Windows 2.0, an improved version of the Windows operating system.

Windows 3.0

A further improved version of Windows was released in 1990, called Windows 3.0. The new operating system took advantage of the speed offered by new computers to present colorful graphics. It was also able to run programs faster than previous versions could, and it was easier to use. It sold more than 10 million copies, making it the company's highest-selling product yet.

Windows 3.0 was an enormous success when it was released in 1990.

Microsoft's Many Products

Microsoft is most famous for its powerful, easy-to-use operating systems. However, the company has produced a wide range of other products throughout its history. Here are a few of Microsoft's greatest hits:

Microsoft Office

In 1989, Microsoft began selling several of its work-related programs in a single package. The first version of Office contained three programs: one for writing text, called Word; the spreadsheet program Excel; and PowerPoint, which allows users to create presentations. More recent versions of Office also contain programs for checking e-mail, managing databases, and other useful tasks.

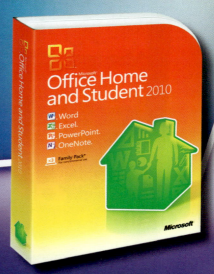

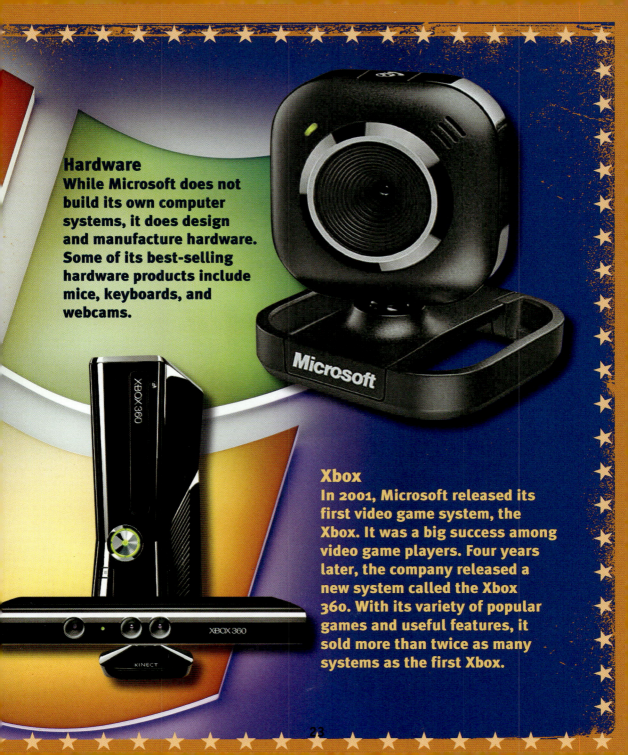

Hardware

While Microsoft does not build its own computer systems, it does design and manufacture hardware. Some of its best-selling hardware products include mice, keyboards, and webcams.

Xbox

In 2001, Microsoft released its first video game system, the Xbox. It was a big success among video game players. Four years later, the company released a new system called the Xbox 360. With its variety of popular games and useful features, it sold more than twice as many systems as the first Xbox.

Melinda French was hired at Microsoft not long after she completed her master's degree.

CHAPTER 3

Meeting Melinda

In 1987, Bill Gates attended a business dinner along with other Microsoft employees. There, he found himself seated next to a young employee named Melinda French. Melinda had only been working at Microsoft for four months. However, her famous new boss did not intimidate her. The two struck up a conversation, beginning a relationship that would last for years to come.

Singer Willie Nelson performed at the Gateses' wedding.

Younger Days

Melinda was born in Dallas, Texas, on August 15, 1964. Like Bill, she became interested in math and computers at a young age and was a fast learner. When she was 14 years old, her father, Ray, purchased an Apple II computer for the family. The machine fascinated Melinda. She began spending long hours learning how to use it.

Apple Computer, Inc., first sold the Apple II computer in 1977.

26

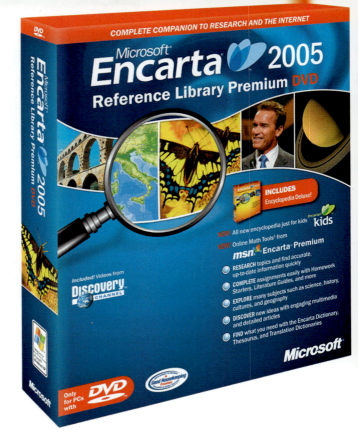

The Encarta encyclopedia, overseen for a time by French, was produced well into the 2000s.

Onward and Upward

French's interest in computers continued into college. She attended Duke University, where she majored in computer science and economics. This course of study allowed her to improve her knowledge of computers while developing important business skills. After graduating in 1986, she stayed at Duke for an extra year to earn a master's degree in business. After finishing, she found work at Microsoft overseeing multimedia projects such as the Encarta CD-ROM encyclopedia.

The Gateses held a reception in Seattle, Washington, several days after their private wedding in Hawaii.

A Perfect Match

Several weeks after their first meeting, Bill asked Melinda out on a date. She accepted, though the two had trouble finding time in their busy work schedules. After almost six years of dating, they finally decided to get married.

Their wedding was held on January 1, 1994, in Hawaii. Old friends such as Paul Allen and billionaire investor Warren Buffett attended the ceremony.

First Steps

Melinda encouraged Bill to use more of his money to support those in need. Soon after their marriage, the couple started the William H. Gates **Foundation**. It was named after Bill's father, who ran the foundation's day-to-day business. The foundation focused mainly on technology in the northwestern United States. One of its projects was to provide public Internet access for people who could not afford their own computers.

William Gates II, Bill Gates's father, helps run the William H. Gates Foundation.

A Major Milestone

Microsoft celebrated its 20th anniversary in 1995. What began with two young men programming in a college dorm room had become one of the world's largest, most powerful companies. That year, Microsoft released Windows 95. Within five weeks, the new operating system was a hit, selling more than seven million copies. Gates also released what became a

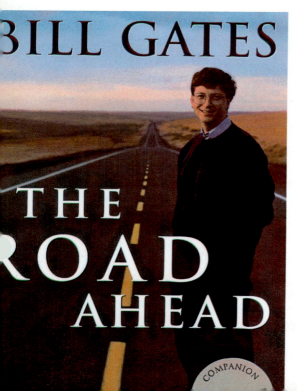

best-selling book, *The Road Ahead*. It detailed his predictions of how technology would affect the world in the future.

Gates's book, much like his software, was a big seller when it was released in 1995.

One of Melinda Gates's last major projects at Microsoft was Microsoft Bob, a program designed to make Windows easier to use.

Starting a Family

The following year, Bill and Melinda celebrated the birth of their first child, a daughter they named Jennifer. By this time, Melinda had worked her way up at Microsoft. Despite her career success, she decided it was important to have an active role in raising her baby. She quit her job when Jennifer was born. However, Melinda was far from retired. She decided to spend more time concentrating on **philanthropy**.

The Gates Library
Foundation
helped provide
computers, Internet
connections,
and software to
libraries.

CHAPTER 4

New Challenges

In 1997, Bill and Melinda launched a second charity. They named it the Gates Library Foundation. The foundation was dedicated to improving the quality of resources offered by public libraries throughout the United States. Bill and Melinda believed that computers and the Internet would be an important part of libraries in the years to come. With this in mind, the foundation focused on making sure libraries had up-to-date technology.

The Gates Foundation has invested about $4 billion to help students prepare for college.

Over time, Bill and Melinda realized the Library Foundation's most useful function was providing resources for students preparing for college. In 1999, they renamed it the Gates Learning Foundation to reflect this new focus.

That same year, they started the Gates Millennium Scholars program. This program set aside $1 billion in college **scholarships** for low-income and **minority** students. Their second child, a son named Rory, was also born in 1999.

The Gates Millennium Scholars program presented its first scholarships in June 2000.

A New Direction

In 2000, Bill announced that he would be stepping down from his position as **CEO** of Microsoft. Longtime Microsoft employee Steve Ballmer, a friend of Bill's from Harvard, would take his place. This didn't mean that Bill was leaving the company, though. He gave himself a new title: chief software architect. He would focus more on creating new products than on running the business.

The Next Step

Later that year, Bill and Melinda decided to take their philanthropy to a new level. They wanted to start focusing more on major global issues, such as finding cures for diseases and ending world hunger. Their three existing foundations were combined to form a new organization called the Bill and Melinda Gates Foundation. The foundation included new programs supporting health and economic development in other nations.

Timeline of the Gateses

1975
Bill Gates and Paul Allen found Microsoft.

1987
Bill Gates and Melinda French meet for the first time.

The Gateses' third child, a daughter named Phoebe, was born in 2002. While raising three children, Bill and Melinda both did their charity work. Bill also continued overseeing new products for Microsoft. In 2006, however, he announced he would take an even smaller role at the company. He said that by 2008, he would be working full-time for the Gates Foundation.

1994

Bill and Melinda get married and start their first charitable organization.

2000

The Gateses combine their various organizations into the Bill and Melinda Gates Foundation.

2006

Warren Buffett promises $30 billion to the Gates Foundation.

Bill Gates and Warren Buffett have both been involved with charities for many years.

CHAPTER 5

Making a Difference

In 2006, the Gates Foundation received its biggest donation yet. When the organization was formed in 2000, it had $17 billion, mostly from the Gates family. Then in 2006, Bill's friend Warren Buffett announced that he was donating $30 billion to the foundation. This more than doubled its funds. It made the Gates Foundation the largest charitable organization in the world.

Gates and Buffett often play the card game bridge together.

Warren Buffett

Like Bill Gates, Warren Buffett has used his business skills to become one of the richest men in the world. Buffett became interested in the stock market as a child. He purchased his first stocks at the age of 11. Now he is considered to be one of the most successful investors of all time, with a personal wealth of more than $60 billion.

The Global Health Program

The Gates Foundation is now organized into three separate programs. Each oversees different kinds of projects. The Global Health Program works with science and technology experts to improve the health of people in poorer countries. It provides resources for scientists to research new cures and **vaccines** for diseases such as malaria and HIV/AIDS. It also works to ensure that such treatments reach the people who need them.

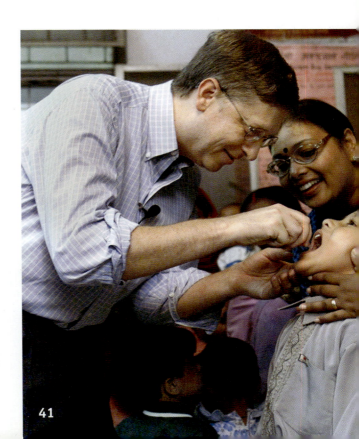

Gates gives a child in India a vaccine against polio, which affects the spine and brain stem.

Tackling the Big Issues

The Global Development Program combats hunger and poverty around the world. The program helps teach farmers how to grow more crops on their land. It also provides clean water to areas without nearby water sources and helps people learn how to manage money.

The United States Program continues the work started by the Gates Learning Foundation. It works to prepare U.S. students for college, offers scholarships, and provides important resources to libraries throughout the nation.

The Global Development Program provides farmers with the tools to grow larger, healthier batches of crops.

Melinda Gates talks with a group of children in New Delhi, India.

The Foundation's Future

Bill and Melinda keep busy overseeing their foundation's many projects. They also travel around the world in search of new challenges and problems they might be able to help solve. Their generosity has brought them acclaim and awards from world leaders around the globe. More importantly, they have used their success in business to make a real impact on the lives of people who need help the most. ★

Amount of money donated to the Gates Foundation by Warren Buffett: $30 billion

Amount of money the Gates Foundation has given away since 1994: $26.2 billion (roughly $3.6 billion through Global Development, $15.3 billion through Global Health, and $6.2 billion through the United States Program, plus more than $1 billion through other projects)

Copies of Windows 95 sold in the first five weeks after release: More than 7 million

Copies of Windows 7 sold every second, one year after release: 7 copies

Number of subscribers to Microsoft's Xbox LIVE online video gaming service (as of 2012): 40 million

Did you find the truth?

F Bill and Melinda Gates started Microsoft together.

T The Bill and Melinda Gates Foundation is the largest charitable foundation in the world.

Resources

Books

Brennan, Patricia. *Who Is Bill Gates?* New York: Grosset & Dunlap, 2013.

Lesinski, Jeanne M. *Bill Gates: Entrepreneur and Philanthropist*. Minneapolis: Twenty-First Century Books, 2009.

Musolf, Nell. *The Story of Microsoft*. Mankato, MN: Creative Education, 2009.

Visit this Scholastic Web site for more information on Bill and Melinda Gates:
★ www.factsfornow.scholastic.com
Enter the keywords **Bill and Melinda Gates**

Important Words

CEO (SEE-EE-OH) — stands for chief executive officer, the person in charge of decision making in a company or organization

foundation (foun-DAY-shuhn) — an organization that provides money to public charities and other worthwhile causes

interface (IN-tur-fase) — a system of interacting with a computer system

license (LYE-suhns) — allow other companies to use a property or product in exchange for money

minority (muh-NOR-i-tee) — a group of people of a particular race, ethnic group, or religion living among a larger group of a different race, ethnic group, or religion

operating system (AH-puh-ray-ting SIS-tuhm) — a master control program on a computer that allows other programs to run on the computer

philanthropy (fuh-LAN-thruh-pee) — the act of helping others by giving time or money to causes and charities

scholarships (SKAH-lur-ships) — money given to students to help them pay for college or follow a course of study

vaccines (vak-SEENZ) — substances that protect people from certain diseases

Index

Page numbers in **bold** indicate illustrations.

About the Author

Josh Gregory writes and edits books for kids. He lives in Chicago, Illinois.